VOLUME 8

SOUTH OF
FRANCE

LES ÉDITIONS
TRANScript
PUBLISHING

ISBN 2-921488-46-9

BORDEAUX

Bordeaux is the wine capital of the world and it has developed a cuisine to match. Yet a practical peasant style of cooking still continues. The result in many dishes is a marriage of hearty country cooking with a sophisticated restaurant style—a thoroughly successful combination.

Unlike most parts of France, regional Bordelais cooking has come chiefly from the city and spread to the surrounding countryside. The city of Bordeaux was a Roman provincial capital and it was the Romans who first planted the grapevines that now ring the city in all directions. In 1152, Bordeaux became the principal port and capital city of England's territories in France. For the next 200 years, the English ruled the area as the Duchy of Aquitaine. Great wealth was brought to the city of Bordeaux as the English popularized Bordeaux wines. In the city of Bordeaux, vineyards overlap the suburbs and whichever way you leave the city,

Cleaning and sorting Bordelais oysters

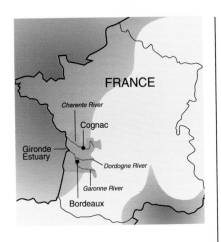

FRANCE

Charente River

Cognac

Gironde Estuary

Dordogne River

Garonne River

Bordeaux

you are at once surrounded by endless rows of neatly-tended vines. To the north and north-west, along the left bank of the Gironde estuary, are the famous Médoc vineyards, and to the south of the city are those of Graves and Entre-Deux-Mers. To the east of Bordeaux are the vineyards of Pomerol and St. Emilion, and along the right bank of the Gironde are the Bourg and Blake vineyards. Oysters from the Gironde are prepared in a number of unusual ways including being stuffed with

shallots in a white wine sauce and being combined with the spicy local sausages. Lamprey, a type of eel, is another Gironde specialty. The best-known method of cooking it is in red wine with leeks and other vegetables.

A specialty of the Gironde that is seldom found outside the area is sturgeon, the caviar-bearing fish that migrates into the estuary in springtime. Sturgeon steaks prepared in various ways have long been a Bordelais specialty, especially when cooked with wine and cream. The local caviar, *créat*, was processed only after the Russian Revolution in 1917, when an emigré from the Czar's empire taught the locals the secrets of preserving sturgeon eggs.

For delicacies other than fish and, of course, wine – the basis of the famous *sauce bordelaise* – the city has to draw upon the resources of the rich areas to the north, south and east of its immediate vicinity. From the light soil of the pine-forested Landes region to the south come delicious vegetables, especially artichokes and potatoes which are often used to garnish local dishes such as *poulet sauté à la bordelaise* and for cepes and mushrooms. From the Landes also come the fatty, corn-fed geese whose livers *(foie gras)* are cooked with grapes or made into pâté de foie gras which is often flavoured with black truffles found in the Dordogne valley region.

Excellent lamb and mutton come from the salt meadows around the town of Pauillac on the left bank of the Gironde. Further north, from vast meadows near the Charente River, come veal and beef. The Charente also flows through a grape-producing area near the town of Cognac where famous brandy of the same name is produced. This fertile river valley also yields plums and the little fragrant, pink-fleshed Charentais melons. ∎

■ GIRONDE ONION SOUP

This version is a bit richer and more refined in flavour than the traditional French onion soup.

- *50 minutes*
- *Serves 6*

**6 large or 12 small onions, thinly
    sliced**
75 g (1/3 cup) chicken fat or lard
good pinch of dried thyme
**salt and freshly ground black
    pepper**
**1.5 L (6 1/2 cups) chicken or veal
    stock**
3 egg yolks
**2.5 mL (1/2 tsp) white wine
    vinegar**
**6 slices French bread, crisped in
    the oven and rubbed with
    1/2 garlic clove**

● Soften the onions in the melted fat in a covered saucepan over very low heat for 15-20 minutes, stirring occasionally.

● When they are soft and translucent but not brown, add the thyme, salt and pepper. Shake the saucepan, add the stock and bring it to the boil. Lower the heat and simmer, covered, for 15-20 minutes.

● Beat the egg yolks until smooth and pale, add the vinegar and beat some more. Gradually whisk in one ladleful of the hot soup.

● Remove the saucepan of soup from the heat and stir in the egg mixture. Keep the soup hot without boiling again, check the seasoning and serve garnished with the crisp French bread slices.

Gironde onion soup

5

■ STUFFED EGGPLANT

- *2 hours*
- *Serves 4*

2 firm eggplants 300 g (11 oz) each
salt and freshly ground black pepper
1 large onion, chopped
60 mL (4 tbls) oil
15 mL (1 tbls) tomato paste
250 g (9 oz) left-over ham or other
  meat, chopped finely
60 mL (4 tbls) white wine (or more
  if desired)
45 mL (3 tbls) breadcrumbs

● Cut off the stalk ends of the eggplants, slice them in half lengthways and make deep criss-cross gashes in the flesh, taking care not to cut through the skins. Sprinkle the cut sides generously with salt and leave them, skin side downwards, for 45 minutes.

● Meanwhile, put the chopped onion in 30 mL (2 tbls) oil in a saucepan over medium heat. Cook until translucent, then stir in the tomato paste followed by the meat. Add the wine, season lightly with salt and pepper and remove from the heat.
● Heat the oven to 190 °C (375 °F). Squeeze the eggplant halves hard to wring out the salty moisture, pat them dry and arrange in an ovenproof dish. Brush the cut surfaces with half the remaining oil.
● Divide the stuffing and press it well down on top of the eggplants to fill the cavities. Sprinkle with breadcrumbs and the rest of the oil. Cover the dish lightly with foil and bake in the oven for about 1 hour.

Serve as an appetizer or a light supper main dish.

- -

■ MUSHROOMS BORDEAUX-STYLE

- *20-25 minutes*
- *Serve 4*

1.25 L (5 cups) cepes, or good-sized
  mushrooms
2 small shallots, or 1 small onion,
  finely chopped
chopped parsley
2 garlic cloves, crushed
60 mL (4 tbls) olive oil
salt and freshly ground black
  pepper
30 mL (2 tbls) lemon juice

● Rinse the cepes or wipe the caps of cultivated mushrooms and pat them dry

with absorbent paper. Remove the stalks. Chop the stalks finely and mix them with the chopped shallots, parsley, crushed garlic and breadcrumbs.
● Put the oil in a large frying-pan and cook the mushroom heads very gently over low heat without browning them or letting them get too soft. When half done, move them with a spatula to the edges of the pan and add the breadcrumb mixture to the centre of the pan.
● Cook the breadcrumb mixture gently for 3-4 minutes, stirring occasionally. Shake the pan, add salt, pepper and lemon juice. Check the seasoning and serve.

■ SCALLOPS BORDEAUX-STYLE

Here is a simple yet unusual way of preparing scallops. Serve them on their own in the shells as a starter. For a light supper dish serve them in a border of piped mashed potato, accompanied by a tossed green salad and the wine opened for cooking.

- *45 minutes*
- *Serves 6 as a starter, 3 as a main course*

450 g (1 lb) scallops
75 mL (1/3 cup) butter
6 green onions, finely chopped
45 mL (3 tbls) cognac
15 mL (1 tbls) tomato paste
1 small garlic clove, crushed
salt and freshly ground black
**   pepper**
6 L (1/4 cup) white Bordeaux wine

● Rinse the scallops quickly in cold water, pat them dry. Slice them horizontally into 2.

● Melt the butter in a small saucepan over low heat and cook the shallots gently until soft and translucent.

● Add the scallops, turning up the heat very slightly so that the butter sizzles; cook them for 4-5 minutes. Meanwhile, warm the cognac in a soup ladle, light it and pour it gradually over the scallops, shaking the pan.

● To the tomato paste and crushed garlic, add a little salt and pepper and the white wine, and allow the mixture to simmer for 6-7 minutes, stirring gently.

● Wash 4 large seashells in hot water. Transfer the scallops to the warmed shells or a serving dish and keep them warm. Raise the heat under the saucepan to reduce the liquid slightly. Strain the sauce over the scallops and serve.

Scallops Bordeaux-style

■ GRILLED STEAK with RED WINE SAUCE

Most good butchers have marrow bones and will saw one into manageable pieces from which marrow – essential for the flavour of the sauce – is easily extracted.

- *5 hours soaking the marrow, plus 1 hour*
- *Serves 2*

1 soup bone cut in large rounds
2 rib steaks about 2.5 cm (1 in) thick
few drops of olive oil
salt and freshly ground black pepper
75 mL (1/3 cup) butter
3 green onions, finely minced
250 mL (1 cup) red wine
1 bay leaf
1 sprig thyme or 5 mL (1 tsp) dried thyme
60 mL (1/4 cup) flour
250 mL (1 cup) beef broth
5 mL (1 tbls) chopped parsley

● Soak the bone segments for 5 hours in cold water. Drain, cover with fresh cold water, put over medium heat and poach for about 15 minutes, never letting the water boil. Drain again, and when cool enough, scoop out the marrow with a round-ended knife or small teaspoon. Dice and reserve 60 mL (1/4 cup) marrow, keeping it warm.

● Lightly brush the steaks with oil; salt and pepper them on both side and reserve while preparing the sauce.

● Heat the oven to broil. Combine the shallots, thyme, bay leaf and wine in a small pan and cook over low heat until the shallots are completely soft and the wine has reduced by half.

● In another small saucepan, melt 25 mL (1 1/2 tbls) butter. Sprinkle with the flour and stir until the flour is golden. Gradually add the broth and bring to the boil stirring constantly. Cook over low heat for 10 minutes. Remove the thyme sprig if necessary and bay leaf from the wine mixture. Pour into the broth mixture. Add salt and pepper and cook over low heat 10 minutes.

● Grill the steaks 3-4 minutes per side. Meanwhile, cut the remaining butter into little pieces and beat them one by one into the warm sauce so that it blends into a creamy sauce without completely melting. Add the marrow and the parsley, pour the sauce over the steaks; serve at once.

Serve with a red Bordeaux. A full-bodied St-Émilion would be a good choice.

■ BEANS in TOMATO SAUCE

- *Beans overnight soaking, then 2 hours*
- *Serves 4*

250 mL (1 cup) dried haricot beans, rinsed and soaked overnight in cold water
60 mL (4 tbls) oil
salt
1 onion, chopped
1 can - 396 mL (14 oz) tomatoes, drained and chopped
pinch of thyme
pinch of crumbled bay leaf
pinch of nutmeg
15 mL (1 tbls) chopped parsley
freshly ground black pepper

● Drain the beans. Heat 45 mL (3 tbls) oil in a saucepan, tip the beans into it and stir to coat them all with oil.

● Cover the beans with cold water and bring to the boil. Lower the heat and allow them to simmer gently, covered, for 1 1/2 hour, adding more water as necessary. Five minutes before they are done, add salt.

● Meanwhile, heat the rest of the oil in another saucepan over low heat and sauté the onions until soft but not coloured. Add the tomatoes, thyme, bay leaf and nutmeg. Season to taste. Cover and cook over very low heat for about 30 minutes.

● Drain the beans, add them to the tomato sauce. Cook them gently for a further 10 minutes, check the seasoning, sprinkle with parsley and serve.

■ SAUTÉED CHICKEN with ARTICHOKE HEARTS

It is the garnish of artichokes and potatoes, one of the hallmarks of Bordelais cuisine, that makes this a special dish worthy of a dinner party.

• *1 hour 30 minutes*
• *Serves 6*

1.5 kg (3 1/4 lb) fresh chicken, cut in 6 serving pieces
75 mL (1/3 cup) vegetable oil
75 mL (1/3 cup) butter
30 mL (2 tbls) tomato paste
2 garlic cloves, crushed
125 mL (1/2 cup) chicken stock
200 mL (7/8 cup) white Bordeaux wine
salt and freshly ground black pepper
2 potatoes, peeled and sliced into thin rounds
2 onions, thinly sliced
400 g (14 oz) canned artichoke hearts, drained and sliced

● Heat 45 mL (3 tbls) oil and 25 g (1 oz) butter in a broad-based saucepan over medium-high heat. Sauté the chicken portions until browned on all sides.

● Stir in the tomato paste and crushed garlic, add the stock and wine and bring to the boil. Add the seasoning, cover and allow to simmer for about 40 minutes.

● Cut the potatoes in half lengthways and then slice thinly. In a heavy frying-pan, heat the remaining 30 mL (2 tbls) of oil and another 25 mL (1 1/2 tbls) of the butter. Add the potato and onion rings

and allow them to cook gently, stirring from time to time, carefully turning the potatoes in the oil and butter. Season with salt and pepper.

● Put the sliced artichoke hearts in a small saucepan with the remaining 25 mL (1 1/2 tbls) butter over very low heat, turning them occasionally to prevent them from burning.

● When the chicken is tender, transfer the portions with a slotted spoon to a serving dish and keep them warm in the oven. Check the seasoning in the sauce and remove it from the heat. Arrange the potatoes, onions and artichokes around the chicken portions to make an attractive border.

● Skim any excess fat off the sauce and heat it up. Coat the dish with the sauce and turn up the oven for a few minutes to heat the dish through thoroughly. (It can be covered with foil and left to heat more slowly, if convenient.)

Serve it with the same wine as that used in cooking, such as an Entre-Deux-Mers.

■ ANISETTE CRÊPES

The addition of Marie Brizard anisette, the local aniseed-flavoured liqueur, gives this dessert a unique flavour.

* *2 hours for batter including resting, then 45 minutes*
* *Serves 4*

350 mL (1 1/2 cup) flour
250 mL (1 cup) sugar
pinch of salt
45 mL (3 tbls) melted butter
2 eggs
350 mL (1 1/2 cup) milk
15 mL (1 tbls) oil
60 mL (4 tbls) anisette
oil or melted butter for greasing

● Combine the flour, sugar and salt in a bowl and make a well in the centre.
● Beat the egg and milk together and pour them into the well. Add the melted butter and the oil and then half of the anisette, gradually whisking them all together with a fork. Continue whisking until all the flour is incorporated into the thin-creamy liquid. Cover with a clean cloth and leave to rest for 2 or more hours.
● Transfer the batter to a jug for easier pouring. Heat a 12-15 cm (5-6 in) diameter frying-pan, then carefully rub it with a thick wad of absorbent paper smeared with oil or melted butter.
● Pour in 15-30 mL (1-2 tbls) of batter (enough to thinly coat the bottom of the pan) and place the pan over medium-high heat. When little air bubbles start to form on the surface, flip it over with a flexible knife blade. Do not overcook. Keep warm until the rest are cooked.
● Put the crêpes on a large, warmed heat-proof serving dish. Heat the remaining anisette. Ignite and pour the flaming liquid on the crêpes. Lift them with a spatula to let the alcohol burn completely.
Serve at once.

Anisette crêpes

■ ALMOND CREAM

The light Bordelais custard makes an excellent end to a rich meal.
You can sprinkle over dark brown sugar, if desired, when serving.

• *2 hours including cooling*
• *Serves 6*

2 large eggs, separated
500 mL (2 cups) milk
75-90 mL (5-6 tbls) flour
45 mL (3 tbls) sugar
salt
8 almonds, blanched and peeled
butter for greasing
a few drops almond extract
sponge fingers sprinkled with
    cognac (optional)

● Beat the egg yolks with 45 mL (3 tbls) of the milk and reserve. Sift the flour, sugar and salt; beat them into the egg yolks.

● Grind the almonds in a food processor, blender or electric coffee mill. Add them to the rest of the milk and bring to the boil. Remove the milk from the heat and stir into the flour mixture with the almond extract and leave to cool. Heat the oven to 200 °C (400 °F).

● Beat the egg whites with a pinch of salt until they are stiff but not dry. Fold the whites into the milk mixture.

● Pour the custard into a buttered soufflé dish, stand the dish in a baking tin and fill the tin with warm water to 25 mm (1 in) from the top. Bake for 35 minutes or until a knife stuck through the middle comes out slightly damp.

> Serve warm with sponge
> fingers sprinkled with cognac.

PROVENCE

Provençal cooking is rooted firmly in the warm climate and history of the region. Its main flavouring ingredients – tomatoes, garlic, olive oil and herbs – find their way into mouth-watering specialties such as garlic mayonnaise and ratatouille.

Of the French regions bordering on the Mediterranean, Provence is most like the travel brochure's image of the south of France. It is a land of fiercely sunlit fields and of pine-dotted slopes where vineyards and olive and lemon groves flourish. The air is scented with wild lavender, rosemary, thyme and fennel. In walled hilltop villages, courtyards are bright with pink and purple bougainvillea and oleander flowers, and from tiny village squares you often catch glimpses of the Mediterranean lapping the coastline.

The origins of Provençal cookery go back to the ancient Greeks and Romans

Gardens rich with flowers and trees beside a hilltop village in Provence

13

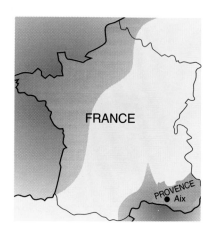

FRANCE

PROVENCE
● Aix

varieties of fish (from the little anchovy upwards), succulent young fruit and vegetables, olive oil, herbs and wines. At its simplest there are the unique Provençal ways with grilled fish; brushing the fish with a branch of thyme soaked in olive oil, or flaming it with dried fennel. On a more sophisticated level are the preserved fruit of Apt, Avignon and Nyons, the almond sweets *(calissons)* of Aix and the nougats of Montélimar.

Other typical specialties include the pungent garlic mayonnaise, *aïoli*, served as an accompaniment to classic fish soups like *bouillabaisse* and *bourride* and also to meat, especially lamb, and vegetables. *Aïoli* is so much a part of Provençal cooking that the traditional Friday (a fat day) meal was named after this creamy-yellow sauce. The stuffed tripe of Marseilles, France's biggest and most ancient port, the smoked sausage of Arles and the famous creamed salt cod dish, *brandade* of Nîmes are also famous. ■

who established the olives and the vines over the hills and made use of the aromatic wild herbs to flavour their fish and meat. Later these traditions were adapted and modified by the French, who in turn, introduced them to more northerly parts of the country so that Provençal cookery has become a major influence on all French cooking. Provençal cooking uses many

Provençal salad

■ RATATOUILLE

- *1 hour salting vegetables,
  then 1 hour 30 minutes*
- *Serves 6-8*

**3 large eggplants, halved
   lengthways
3 large zucchinis, halved
   lengthways
salt and freshly ground black
   pepper
150 mL (1/2 cup) olive oil
3 large onions, sliced in thin rings
60 mL (4 tbls) tomato purée
4 garlic cloves, chopped
3 large green or red peppers,
   seeded and cut into thin strips
5 large tomatoes, blanched,
   skinned and chopped, or
   400 g (14 oz) canned tomatoes,
   well-drained
small pinch of cinnamon
pinch of dried basil
pinch of dried thyme**

● Cut the eggplants and zucchinis across into slices about 2.0 cm (3/4 in) thick. Place them in layers in a colander, sprinkling each layer with salt. Top them with a weighted plate and drain the vegetables for 1 hour.

● Heat the olive oil gently in a broad, heavy pan over low heat and cook the onions in it. When they are (transparent about 15 minutes) stir in the tomato purée and allow the mixture to cook for 3-4 minutes, stirring occasionally.

● Dry the eggplants and zucchinis with absorbent paper and stir them into the pan. Add the garlic and the peppers, shake the pan, cover and let it simmer for about 10 minutes.

● Add the tomatoes, thyme, bay leaf, cinnamon, basilic, salt and stir once or twice and leave to cook for a further 40-45 minutes. Remove the lid for the final few minutes to let the sauce reduce if the dish seems too liquid. Check the seasoning before serving.

Ratatouille

● ●

■ VEGETABLE and AÏOLI HORS D'OEUVRE

To succeed in preparing aïoli, it is essential that the egg yolks, oil and mixing bowls are all at room temperature.

- *15 minutes for the vegetables, plus 15-20 minutes for the aïoli*
- *Serves 4-6*

500 mL (2 cups) young French beans, topped, tailed and blanched

1 small cauliflower, cored and cut into florets

5 young carrots, cut into 7.5 cm (3 in) matchsticks

3 zucchinis, cut into 7.5 cm (3 in) long matchsticks, dusted with salt and left to sweat while making the *aïoli*

■ FOR THE AÏOLI
3-5 garlic cloves

Vegetable and aïoli hors d'oeuvre

• •

2.5-4 mL (1/2-3/4 tsp) salt
2 egg yolks, at room temperature
250 mL (1 cup) olive oil, at room
    temperature
5 mL (1 tsp) lemon juice
pinch of freshly ground white
    pepper

● Crush the peeled garlic cloves and
mash them to a paste with the salt. Tip
the egg yolks into the bowl and combine
them thoroughly with the garlic and salt,
using a wire whisk or rotary beater.

● Drop by drop, add the oil, beating
thoroughly after each addition. When
the mixture has emulsified and looks
glossy, add the oil a little faster, but
resist the urge to add too much oil, or the
mixture will separate. When mayonnaise
becomes too thick to stir easily, beat in
5-10 mL (1-2 tsp) tepid water.

● When all the oil has been incorporated,
beat in the lemon juice and pepper. Pour
the sauce into a small serving bowl in the
centre of a platter, rinse and wipe the
zucchinis dry and surround the bowl with
the vegetables.

If the aïoli separates while you are making
it, take a clean bowl and crush a fresh
garlic clove in it with a pinch of salt. Add
another egg yolk and gradually beat in
the separated aïoli, then the rest of the oil.

Like other mayonnaises, aïoli keeps
well in the refrigerator for 3-4 days. It is
advisable to cover it tightly in cling film
and then enclose the whole bowl in a
sealed polythene bag or its pungency
could easily affect every other food in
the refrigerator.

■ SALADE AIXOISE

• *30-40 minutes*
• *Serves 4-5*

4 potatoes, cut into pieces
500 mL (2 cups) green beans,
    sliced into thin strips with
    the ends cut off
30 mL (2 tbls) wine vinegar
75 mL (5 tbls) olive oil
4 tomatoes, cut into 4
2 hard-boiled eggs, cut into 4
1 pinch tarragon
8 to 12 anchovy fillets, drained
8 to 12 black olives, pitted
2 pickles, cut into pieces

■ FOR THE DRESSING
75 mL (3 fl oz) olive oil
30 mL (1 fl oz) wine vinegar
salt and freshly ground black pepper

● Wash the potatoes, place them in a
saucepan, cover with cold water and bring
to the boil. Salt and cook for 20-25 minutes
until tender. Once cooked, peel and cut into
rounds about 5 mm (1/4 in) in thickness.
● Cook the green beans in boiling water
for 5-7 minutes after the boiling has
resumed. Drain, rinse under cold water,
and drain again.
● To make the vinaigrette, mix together
2 pinches of salt, 1 good pinch of pepper
and the vinegar in a bowl. Add the oil
and beat with a fork until well mixed.
● Place the potatoes, green beans and
tomatoes in a large salad bowl. Add the
tarragon, sprinkle with the vinaigrette and
gently toss, being careful not to break the
green bean slices. Lay the anchovy fillets
diagonally across the top and decorate
with the olives, egg and pickle.

■ BRAISED BEEF

One of the most ancient and traditional of Provençal dishes, this beef stews is good, if not better, when gently reheated. As it freezes well, it is worth doubling.

- *7 hours*
- *Serves 6*

1.2 kg (2 1/2 lb) braising steak, cut into chunks about 75 g (3 oz) each
1 calf or pig's foot split lengthways or a pig's knuckle
250 g (8 oz) streaky unsmoked bacon, cut across into strips
2 large onions, coarsely chopped
60 mL (4 tbls) olive oil
5 tomatoes, blanched, peeled, seeded and coarsely chopped or 396 mL (14 oz) canned tomatoes, drained, seeded and chopped
1 medium-sized onion, wrapped around with a strip of orange zest held in place by 5 cloves
2 large carrots, split lengthways
4 garlic cloves, peeled
a fresh bouquet garni made from a sprig of thyme and parsley and a bay leaf tied together with string

Braised beef

600 mL (2 1/2 cups) or more red wine
salt and freshly ground black pepper

● Heat the oven to 150 °C (300 °F). Cook the chopped onions in the olive oil over moderate heat in a heavy, flameproof casserole with a close-fitting lid until soft. Continue cooking for 5 minutes, then remove from the heat and allow the mixture to cool a little, 5-10 minutes.

● Place the orange-wrapped onion stuck with the cloves in the centre of the casserole. Lay the split carrots over the bottom. Distribute the garlic cloves evenly, and sprinkle the bacon strips over them. Arrange the two halves of calf's foot, pig's trotter or knuckle, on either side of the whole onion and place the meat chunks all around them, tucking the bouquet garni into the centre. Pour in the red wine to cover and sprinkle with plenty of pepper.

● Cover the dish closely with foil and then with a lid, bring it to the boil over moderate heat. Reduce the heat and simmer for about 10 minutes.

● Put the casserole in the oven for 6 hours, checking towards the end that the liquid is adequate, adding hot water or broth if necessary. Just before serving, add the salt and more pepper to taste. Serve the beef with boiled noodles or macaroni and a green salad.

If more convenient, prepare the dish in advance up to the point where it is covered with wine. Keep it in a cool place to marinate for up to 8 hours before cooking.

■ CREAMED SALT COD

• *12 hours soaking fish, plus 1 hour*
• *Serves 4-5*

700 g (1 1/2 lb) salt cod, in pieces, smoked cod or fresh cod fillets
300 mL (1 1/4 cup) olive oil, from a bottle warmed in a saucepan of hot water
250 mL (1 cup) 35% cream, warmed
8-10 rounds of French bread, lightly fried in olive oil

● If using, soak the salt cod in a bowl of cold water for 10-12 hours, changing the water 4-5 times.
● Rinse the cod, place it in a large saucepan and cover with cold water. Bring the liquid to the boil, then lower the heat so that the surface barely shivers. Poach the fish for 10 minutes.
● Drain the fish, refresh it under cold water, and flake the flesh off the skin and bone, discarding the latter.
● Pour a 60 mL (4 tbls) oil into a saucepan and mash the fish with a wooden spoon into the oil.
● Continue to mash, gradually incorporating the remaining warmed oil and cream into the fish mixture, adding about 30 mL (2 tbls) of each ingredient in turn. Never allow the mixture to simmer – this dish should be warm but not hot.
● When all the liquid has been absorbed and the mixture is the consistency of creamy mashed potatoes, add salt and pepper to taste. Fry the bread rounds. Turn the creamed cod onto a warmed dish surrounded with the fried bread, and serve at once with a mixed salad.

■ PROVENÇAL FISH SOUP

Bourride *is one of the oldest of Provençal recipes — perhaps 200 years old – and it can be varied greatly. One essential ingredient, however, is the celebrated Provençal garlic and egg yolk sauce,* aïoli *– without it,* bourride *is simply a fish soup.*

- *1 hour 30 minutes plus time for making the* aïoli
- *Serves 6-8*

1.5 kg (3 lb) white fish, such as cod, halibut, brill cut in pieces
60 mL (1/4 cup) oil
1 large onion, chopped
2 thick slices of fresh fennel
1 large tomato, chopped
1 large carrot, cleaned and sliced
1 leek, cleaned and sliced
10 mL (2 tsp) dried thyme
1 bay leaf
a few sprigs of parsley
1.5 cm (1/2 in) wide strip of lemon or orange peel
750 mL (3 cups) dry white wine
3 egg yolks
a few drops of lemon juice
250 mL (1 cup) or more of *aïoli*
6-8 slices French bread, lightly toasted

● Soften the onion, fennel and tomato gently in the oil in the large saucepan over low heat. When they are soft, add the other vegetables, the garlic, the herbs, the citrus peel and the fish pieces, and pour in the wine and 750 mL (3 cups) water.

● Bring the liquid to the boil gradually, then cover the pan and let it simmer for 30-45 minutes.

● Remove the soup from the heat and strain the fish. Strain the liquid into a bowl through a conical sieve, pressing down firmly on the solids to extract all the flavour.

● Put the egg yolks into another saucepan, large enough to contain all the soup, and whisk them together with the lemon juice and 45 mL (3 tbls) of *aïoli*. Add a ladleful of the hot soup, whisking all time, and then add the rest of the soup, still whisking. Add salt and pepper to taste.

● Gently reheat the *bourride* without allowing it to boil. To serve, ladle the soup into warmed bowls, then float a slice of lightly toasted bread, topped with a mound of *aïoli*, in each bowl of soup. Serve the fish separately.

● ●

■ PROVENÇAL ANCHOVY SAUCE

- *Cooking time for the lamb, then 10 minutes*
- *Makes about 125 mL (4 fl oz)*

10 anchovy fillets, finely chopped
175 mL (3/4 cup) parsley, finely chopped
juice of 1 lemon

● Roast, fry or grill the lamb in the usual way, set it on a serving dish and keep warm. Skim the fat from the pan juices. Stir the anchovy fillets, parsley, and lemon juice into the pan juices, add a little water and scrape the pan well. Simmer the liquid over medium heat for 1-2 minutes and pour into a warmed sauceboat.

● ●

■ SAUTÉED CHICKEN

- *1 hour 15 minutes*
- *Serves 4-5*

1.5 kg (3 1/4 lb) chicken, cut into serving pieces
6-8 slices unsmoked back bacon, one for each chicken portion
10 mL (2 tsp) dried thyme
60 mL (4 tbls) olive oil
1 large onion, roughly chopped
2 garlic cloves, chopped finely
3 large tomatoes, blanched, skinned, seeded and chopped
500 mL (2 cups) dry white wine
salt and freshly ground black pepper
150 g (5 oz) black olives, pitted and halved
75 mL (1/3 cup) parsley, chopped

● Sprinkle each chicken portion with a pinch of dried thyme and wrap in a slice of bacon. Secure the bacon with a toothpick, stiching it so that the stick lies along the side of the packet.

● Put the olive oil in a wide flameproof casserole over medium heat and fry the portions on both sides until lightly cooked.

● Add the onions, garlic and tomatoes, and pour in the white wine. Simmer the mixture, covered, for about 25 minutes.

● Remove the lid from the pan, season with salt and pepper, and cook for 8-10 minutes longer over slightly higher heat to let the sauce reduce. Add the black olives, sprinkle with the parsley and serve.

Sautéed chicken

■ PROVENÇAL SPINACH FLAN

*In this very traditional sweet from Nice, spinach is the unusual ingredient. Pâte brisée is
French for "shortcrust" and is a special French tart pastry which always includes sugar.*

* 10 minutes plus 1 hour, resting for pastry
  plus 2 hours 30 minutes
* Serves 6

**450 g (1 lb) spinach, trimmed and
  cooked or 200 g (7 oz) frozen
  spinach, cooked
the grated zest of 1 lemon
pinch of salt
1 medium-sized egg, beaten
crystallized orange slices (optional)**

**■ FOR THE PÂTE BRISÉE
350 mL (1 1/2 cup) flour
1 pinch of salt
25 mL (1 1/2 tbls) sugar
30-45 mL (2-3 tbls) iced water
100 mL (3/8 cup) unsalted butter,
  diced small**

**■ FOR THE CRÈME PÂTISSIÈRE
3 egg yolks
1 mL (1/4 tsp) salt
20 mL (4 tsp) flour, sifted
125 mL (1/2 cup) vanilla sugar or
  plain sugar + a few drops
  vanilla extract
250 mL (1 cup) 15% cream,
  warmed over low heat
5 mL (1 tsp) butter**

● To make the *pâte brisée*, sift the flour
with the salt and sugar. Rub the butter
with your fingertips into the flour mixture,
sprinkle in cold water and pull the pastry
together with a fork. Use your hands to

make the pastry into a ball. Knead it
briefly by pressing it with heel of your
hand and then forming it into a ball
again. Wrap it in cling film and
refrigerate for at least 1 hour.
● Heat the oven to 200 °C (400 °F).
Roll out the chilled pastry and line a
19 cm (7 1/2 in) flan tin with it. Wrap
the extra dough in cling film and save
for decoration. Prick the base all over
with a fork, line it with greaseproof paper
or foil and fill with dried beans. Bake
for 10-12 minutes, remove the foil and
beans and cool the half-cooked pastry.
Turn the oven to 190 °C (375 °F).
● Meanwhile, make the *crème pâtissière*.
Whisk the egg yolks with the salt in a
small, heavy-based saucepan. When
they are smooth and creamy, beat in the
sifted flour and the sugar over low heat.
● Pour in the hot cream, gradually, still
beating the mixture. Allow it to come to
the boil, stirring continually with a wooden
spoon. Let it bubble over low heat for
1 minute, stirring briskly. Remove from
heat and blend in the butter.
● Drain the spinach very well, then
stir it into the crème pâtissière with the
lemon zest and salt. Pour this into the
pastry shell.
● Decorate the top with thin strips
cut from the remaining pastry. Glaze
with the beaten egg, and bake for
30-35 minutes. Serve hot or cold,
decorated with the crystallized orange
slices.

LANGUEDOC

This sun-baked province on the Mediterranean in the south-west of France is most famous as the home of the *cassoulet*, the *carbonnade* and the *daube*, but there is also an abundant supply of game, mountain lamb, sea and freshwater fish, vegetables and fruit to produce a rich and exciting variety of dishes.

The Languedoc is a huge and sweeping crescent-shaped segment of south-western France, bordered by the Mediterranean along its inner curve and extending from the foothills of the Pyrenees in the south as far east as the banks of the River Rhône. Its name comes from the ancient language of the south, the "langue d'oc," which is still spoken by some country people as it has been – with variations

– almost since Roman times. Legacies of these bygone civilizations still remain among the undulating landscapes of the Languedoc. In some former Roman cities like Narbonne, Albi and Carcassonne, only traces of this classical past remain, but on Roman foundations throughout the region have risen wonderful medieval streets and walled strongholds, great monuments and churches basking in the sun.

This sun, that so warms and bathes green mountainsides and sandy coastal strips alike in its brilliant light, is perhaps responsible for the region's local nickname, "le Midi" or the "high noon" of France. Certainly the climate is largely responsible for the richness of produce to be found all over the Languedoc: wines

A street market in Languedoc

from the shapely hills of Minervois, the valleys of the Aude and the lower Rhône; beautiful early vegetables like asparagus and artichokes; a particularly flavoursome garlic, many varieties of wild mushrooms and herbs that are rare; and a highly prized delicacy, the aromatic truffle. An abundance of delicious fruit grows here, from plums and apricots and grapes to strawberries, oranges and figs, plus groves of olives and millions of almond trees.

Livestock is equally plentiful, from the mountain lamb and mutton to the veal and beef of the pasture lands and the backyard pig. Game there is in plenty, such as izard (mountain goat), hare and wild rabbit, partridge, teal and wood pigeon. Domestic poultry is a succulent specialty of the region – fat capons, geese, ducks and turkeys all feature in local recipes and their carefully fattened livers are reserved for making the famous *pâtés* and terrines.

As well as the numerous types of fish hauled from the Mediterranean (including tuna in the late spring) and the shellfish cultivated in the salt lakes, the Languedoc rejoices in a good variety of freshwater fish that are native to its many streams and rivers: tench, bream, perch, pike and shad as well as river trout. Fat frogs and ponderous snails inhabit damp areas near running water and contribute to the pleasure of eating in the Languedoc.

Culinary traditions go back a long way in this part of France and derive from legacies of invaders and migrant peoples. That supreme achievement of Languedoc cooking, the garlicky, bean-based *cassoulet*, very possibly originated from a Roman dish that combined mutton and white haricot beans although, after generations of additions and refinements, an ancient Roman might find it hard to identify this simpler concoction. But the *cassoulet* continues to be regarded with great respect throughout the region: small family businesses have been known to close their doors for a whole day in order to concentrate properly on its preparation and the rival merits of the versions associated with Carcassonne, Castelnau, Castelnaudary and Toulouse are hotly disputed.

If the Romans originated the *cassoulet*, it was the Arabs, spilling over into the Languedoc from neighbouring Spain, who contributed most to the cooking of the region. The use of almonds in various dishes is part of their tradition. Pounded almonds are an ingredients of the sauce that accompanies snails in *escargots à la narbonnaise*, and almonds lend a special flavour to a local bouillabaisse.

Almonds also figure largely (together with orange flower water) in the filling for the traditional sweet flan knowm as *croustade languedocienne* and the huge repertoire of sweetmeats and pastries of which the Languedoc is so proud. Specialties include honey *croquettes*, Limoux cakes, Albi cookies, Carcassonne flaky pastries and crystallized fruits, and the chocolates and *marrons glacés* of Montpellier.

The main dishes most widely enjoyed tend to be substantial and robust despite the heat. Soups like *pot-au-feu carcassonnais* (with ribs of beef) and the fish soups of Sète and Collioure are almost meals in themselves. Meaty fish like tuna and cod are prepared in rich *ragoûts* or stuffed. Tripe, sweetbreads and brains are often cooked in pastry, while mutton and beef are braised for hours as *carbonnades* or *daubes* or are combined with salsify, potatoes, olives, chetnuts, rare mushrooms, and other vegetables as well as the traditional beans. ∎

■ TROUT with CREAM and MUSHROOMS

- *45 minutes*
- *Serves 4*

4 fresh trout, 250 g (8 oz) each, cleaned
salt and freshly ground black pepper
flour
125 mL (1/2 cup) butter
750 mL (3 cups) mushrooms, trimmed and thinly sliced
20 mL (4 tsp) lemon juice
250 mL (1 cup) 35% cream
pinch of dried chervil
mashed potatoes or new potatoes, to serve

● Lightly salt the trout inside and coat them in seasoned flour.

● Melt 45 mL (3 tbls) butter in a saucepan over a low heat, tip in the mushrooms and turn them until slightly and evenly softened, about 3-4 minutes.

Add the lemon juice, season and reserve.

● Choose a flameproof dish into which the trout will fit comfortably side by side. Gently melt the rest of the butter in it and fry the trout for 4 minutes on each side. Distribute the mushrooms and their juices around the fish, pour over the cream, sprinkle on the chervil and raise the heat slightly.

● Heat the oven to broil.

● When the cream is bubbling, remove the dish from the heat and put it quickly under the grill. Continue cooking for about 10 minutes, occasionally basting the exposed sides of the trout to prevent burning.

● Serve when nicely brown, accompanied by fluffy mashed potatoes or plain boiled new potatoes.

Trout with cream and mushrooms

■ CASSOULET CASTELNAUDARY-STYLE

- *8-12 hours soaking, then 5 hours*
- *Serves 8-10*

800 mL (3 1/4 cups) haricot beans, soaked overnight
125 mL (1/2 cup) lard
800 g (1 3/4 lb) goose or duck cut in 6 pieces
6 onions, chopped
6 garlic cloves, crushed
100 mL (3/8 cup) tomato paste
396 mL (14 oz) canned tomatoes
10 mL (2 tsp) paprika
2 mL (1/2 tsp) cayenne pepper
salt and freshly ground black pepper
2 bouquets garnis (thyme, bay leaf, parsley)
500 g (1 lb) lean pork shoulder, cut into 2.5 cm (1 in) cubes
6 shallots, chopped
60 mL (1/4 cup) flour
250 mL (1 cup) light beef stock
stick of cinnamon

Traditional cassoulet

1 large onion, stuck with 6 cloves
1 large carrot
2 whole heads of garlic
500 g (18 oz) salt pork belly, in
**   1 piece**
200 g (7 oz) garlic sausage, in
**   1 piece**
1 extra garlic clove, peeled
6-8 pork sausages
175 mL (3/4 cup) fresh bread
**   crumbs**
crusty French bread, to serve
crisp green salad, to serve

● Melt the lard in a large, heavy-based saucepan over a medium heat, add the duck or goose pieces and fry until golden, 4-5 minutes. Remove the joints and reserve. Pour off three-quarters of the fat and reserve.

● To the fat remaining in the pan, add the chopped onions and crushed garlic and stir for 2-3 minutes over medium heat. Stir in the tomato paste, add the canned tomatoes, paprika, cayenne, salt and 1 of the bouquets garnis. Return the duck or goose pieces to the pan, cover and cook over a low heat for 2 1/2 - 2 3/4 hours.

● In another heavy pan, melt 30 mL (2 tbls) of the reserved fat and lightly fry the cubes of fresh pork. When evenly coloured, add the chopped shallots, sprinkle on the flour, stir for 1-2 minutes, and then gradually add the stock, still stirring. Season with salt and pepper, add the cinnamon stick, cover and simmer gently for 2 - 2 1/2 hours.

● Drain the beans, put in a large saucepan, cover with fresh cold water, add the onion stuck with cloves, the carrot, garlic heads, salt pork and the second bouquet garni. Bring to the boil and simmer for 1 1/2 hour.

● Season the beans with salt, add the garlic sausage and simmer a further 20 minutes.

● Remove the 2 pans containing the meats from the heat, uncover and check the seasoning (it should be rather strong). Reserve.

● Remove the salt pork and garlic sausage from the bean saucepan and set them aside to cool slightly. Drain the beans and discard the onion, carrot, garlic and bouquet garni.

● With a slotted spoon, remove the duck and pork pieces from their respective sauces and set aside. Discard the bouquet garni and the cinnamon stick, and combine both sauces with the drained beans.

● Rub a large earthenware or cast iron casserole with the remaining garlic clove, then spoon a generous layer of the bean mixture into the dish. Lay 2 or 3 pieces of duck or goose on top of the beans, then some of the pork cubes and one thick slice each of the salt pork and garlic sausage. Cover with another layer of beans and repeat the process, finishing with a layer of beans.

● Heat the oven to 230 °C (450 °F).

● Put the remaining reserved fat into a frying-pan and fry the pork sausages until they are three-quarters done. Tuck the sausages into the top layer of beans and sprinkle with fat from the frying-pan and the breadcrumbs.

● Put the casserole near the top of the oven; cook for 20 minutes or until the crumbs are nicely browned and the whole dish well heated through.

● Serve from the casserole with crusty French bread and a crisp green salad.

> *A red Bordeaux, preferably from Prédoc, full bodied but fruity will be nice with this dish.*

■ RUSTIC LIVER TERRINE

- *5-5 hours 30 minutes, plus cooling and chilling*
- *Serves 8*

450 g (1 lb) calf's liver
125 g (4 oz) lean pork
125 g (4 oz) salt pork
250 g (9 oz) chilled lard
250 mL (1 cup) fresh breadcrumbs
100 mL (3/8 cup) chicken stock

60 mL (1/4 cup) dry vermouth
75 mL (1/3 cup) chopped parsley
450 g (1 lb) goose, turkey or
    chicken livers
1 mL (1/4 tsp) mace
1 mL (1/4 tsp) ground cloves
salt and freshly ground black
    pepper
1 bay leaf
3 or 4 mushrooms caps, sliced
flour for sealing

Rustic liver terrine

28

■ TO SERVE
hot toast or French bread

● Chop the calf's liver, lean pork and salt pork and 175 mL (3/4 cup) lard fairly finely (but do not mince – the texture should be rough).

● Soak the breadcrumbs in the stock and vermouth and add to the chopped ingredients. Mix well, adding the parsley, mace, cloves, salt and pepper, and reserve.

● Heat the oven to 150 °C (300 °F).

● Clean and coarsely chop the poultry livers. Pack a layer of the reserved pork and calf's liver mixture into the bottom of a round or oval dish. Cover with a layer of poultry livers. Repeat the process, pressing each layer of mixed ingredients.

● Place a bay leaf in the centre and surround with the mushrooms slices. Top with a thin covering of the rest of the lard and seal on the lid with a flour and water paste.

● Place in a pan of hot water to come halfway up the side of the terrine and cook for 3 1/2 hours.

● Remove from the oven, cool and chill thoroughly. Unmould and wrap the terrine in a "collar" of foil or serve from the dish with hot toast or crusty French bread.

> *Liver terrine should be served with a semi-sweet sparkling wine or a Sauternes.*

■ PEAS with HAM LANGUEDOC-STYLE

• *1 hour 15 minutes*
• *Serves 4*

150 mL (5/8 cup) butter
125 g (4 oz) lean raw ham, chopped (prosciutto or Parma ham)
1 onion, chopped
500 g (1 lb) frozen green peas
100 mL (3/8 cup) flour
1 mL (1/4 tsp) sugar
1 mL (1/4 tsp) salt
bouquet garni (thyme, bay leaf, parsley)
4 slices of bread

● Melt 45 mL (3 tbls) butter in a broad, shallow pan and gently fry the onion and ham for about 10 minutes.

● Add the peas and turn them quickly to mix the ingredients. Sprinkle on the flour, mix thoroughly again and allow to cook for 2 minutes. Add 150 mL (5/8 cup) water, the sugar, salt and bouquet garni. Stir once, cover and simmer for 25 minutes.

● Remove the lid and continue simmering for 10 minutes to allow excess moisture to evaporate. Melt the remaining butter in a frying pan over low heat. Fry the bread slices 5-7 minutes or until crispy.

● Discard the bouquet garni, pile the creamy pea mixture onto the croutons and serve immediately.

■ BRAISED BEEF with WINE and VEGETABLES

- *10-12 hours marinating, then 6 hours*
- *Serves 6-8*

1.5 kg (3 1/4 lb) lean chuck steak, cut in 2.5 cm (1 in) slices
1 L (4 1/2 cups) white wine
45 mL (3 tbls) olive oil
flour
30 mL (2 tbls) beef dripping or lard
250 g (9 oz) unsmoked streaky bacon, cut in 2.5 cm (1 in) pieces
6 shallots, chopped
6 carrots, sliced in 1.5 cm (1/2 in) pieces
4 garlic cloves, halved
375 mL (1 1/2 cup) mushrooms, halved
salt and freshly ground black pepper
bouquet garni (thyme, bay leaf, parsley)
zest of half an orange, cut in a single curl if possible
flour for sealing
75 mL (1/3 cup) chopped parsley

■ TO SERVE
plain boiled rice

● Put the steak in a large bowl and marinate it in the wine and oil, covered, in a cool place for 10-12 hours.

● Remove the meat from the marinade, drain it, pat dry, then dredge with flour and set aside. Reserve the marinade.

● Heat the oven to 180 °C (350 °F).

● Melt the dripping in a deep frying-pan over medium heat and fry the bacon pieces for 3-4 minutes, turning them constantly to prevent sticking. Remove the bacon and reserve.

● In the same pan quickly fry the floured meat lightly on both sides. Remove it from the pan and reserve.

● Tip the shallots, carrots and garlic into the pan, and turn these for 2-3 minutes until evenly coated with the fat and juices.

● Lay the meat slices in a heavy, lidded casserole and surround with the vegetables from the frying-pan and the mushrooms. Pour in the reserved marinade, season with salt and pepper and add the bouquet garni and the orange peel.

● Seal the lid with a flour and water paste and cook in the oven for about 4 1/2 hours.

● Check the seasoning and serve sprinkled with chopped parsley and accompanied with plain boiled rice.

Serve with a red spicy and woodsy Bordeaux.

■ GRAPE TART

- *Making and resting pastry, then
  1 hour 15 minutes*
- *Serves 4-5*

pâte brisée
**450 g (1 lb) large seedless green
  grapes**
flour
a little egg white, for brushing
45 mL (3 tbls) sugar
**60 mL (1/4 cup) quince, apple or
  crab-apple jelly**

● Make the pâte brisée and set aside in
a cool place to rest for at least 1 hour.

● Heat the oven to 190 °C (375 °F).

● Cut the grapes in half. Stand the
grapes, cut side down, on a clean cloth.

● Roll out the pastry and line a 20 cm
(8 in) flan tin with it. Prick the bottom
with a fork, brush with the egg white and
fill with the grapes, pressing them close
together, cut side down. Sprinkle with the
sugar and bake for 35-45 minutes.

● As soon as the tart is baked, heat the
jelly until liquid and brush over the tart.
Serve warm or cold.

Grape tart

■ PANCAKE and APRICOT GÂTEAU

- 24 hours soaking,
  then 2 hours 30 minutes
- Serves 4-5

225 g (8 oz) dried apricots
350 mL (1 1/2 cup) white wine
175 mL (3/4 cup) sugar
15 mL (1 tbls) gelatine
oil for cooking
175 mL (3/4 cup) chopped walnuts
6 half walnuts, for garnish

■ FOR THE CRÊPE BATTER
250 mL (1 cup) flour
2 mL (1/2 tsp) salt
2 eggs
200 mL (7/8 cup) milk
15 mL (1 tbls) vegetable oil

● Put the apricots in a small saucepan, add the wine and soak for 18-24 hours.

● Make the crêpe batter. Sift the flour with the salt into a bowl. In a separate bowl, whisk the eggs, milk and oil together and pour onto the flour, beating constantly until the batter is smooth. Cover it and leave to rest for 2 hours.

● In a small cup, reserve 45 mL (3 tbls) of the wine in which the apricots were soaked. Cut the apricots into strips, return them to the rest of the wine, stir in the sugar and simmer, covered, about 1 1/2 hour, until they are soft.

● Towards the end of the cooking time, soak the gelatine in the reserved wine; when the apricots are soft, stir it into the hot fruit mixture until dissolved. When slightly cooled, purée the mixture in a blender or food processor, return it to its saucepan and reserve.

● Transfer the crêpe batter to a measuring jug. Coat an 18 cm (7 in) diameter frying-pan with a little oil and heat to shimmering point. Pour in 60 mL (1/4 cup) batter, swirl, and cook for about a minute each side. Repeat the process until all the batter is used, making about 10 crêpes, setting them on a wire rack as they are done.

● Not more than 2 hours before serving assemble the "cake." Put 1 crêpe on a plate, cover with a layer of apricot purée and a sprinkling of chopped walnuts. Repeat with the rest of the crêpes, finishing with a layer of purée. Decorate with the walnut halves, cover lightly with baking-paper and leave to stand at room temperature until ready to serve. Slice it with a sharp knife as you would a cake.

FRENCH RIVIERA and CORSICA

The county of Nice, at the heart of France's elegant Côte d'Azur or "Riviera," and the Mediterranean island of Corsica have similar backgrounds and share a tradition of flavourful, colourful cooking. *Ratatouille* and *salade niçoise* have delicious, less famous counterparts in dishes such as *tapenade*, black olive, tuna and anchovy hors d'oeuvres.

Separated by 150 kilometres or so of limpid blue Mediterranean, Nice and the island of Corsica have much more in common than simply Frenchness. Both have the same rugged beauty, with wooded mountains that plunge into the sea in a succession of bays and inlets separated by craggy cliffs. But they share more than just appearances: both were settled by the Greeks and then by the Romans, who terraced the hillsides and introduced olives and vines, and both came under Italian rule during the Middle Ages. Nice and its neighbouring coast belonged to the Kingdom of Savoy, while Corsica was a possession of the Republic of Genoa, and both retain souvenirs of their Italian past in their impressive older buildings, in many

A market in Nice

FRANCE

RIVIERA
Nice •

CORSICA

local words and phrases, and in their cuisine.

In gastronomic terms, Nice and the Riviera share many traditions with Corsica, including more than a hint of their Italian heritage. Both cuisines are based on the olive oil of wonderful quality that is produced in the hills. Both rely for their distinctive flavours on the pungent, sun-dried herbs that grow wild in such profusion. Both make generous use of the local fish, fowl and game, of the diligently cultivated oranges, lemons, almonds, tomatoes and other fruits, nuts and vegetables, and of the heady wines from the vineyards that clothe every fertile slope.

Niçois cooking, thanks to the influence of the aristocratic clientele that formely patronized the hotels and restaurants of the Riviera, is the more refined. *Salade niçoise* and *ratatouille* are both internationally known classics. But the locals still stay faithful to many of their own highly original ways of combining and preparing food: mixing deep-fried sardines with pitted olives, for instance, or stewing veal with anchovy fillets, and making much use of such ingredients as lentils, polenta (corn meal) and chick peas as accompaniments for meat and for other vegetable dishes. Anchovies are staple ingredient used in many ways. In

one, the quickly made hors d'oeuvre, *anchoïade*, anchovy fillets are mashed with oil, garlic and a little vinegar and spread on hot toast.

Other typical Niçois dishes are *pissala*, pickled whitebait, *stoccaficida*, dried cod cooked with tomatoes and potatoes, *lièvre à la niçoise*, hare stewed with sausages, mushrooms and onions, and *pissaladière*, onion flan with anchovy fillets. Desserts are mostly made from local fruits: *fougassettes*, sweet buns flavoured with saffron and orange blossom, candied orange and lemon slices, creamy confections like *charlotte aux framboises* or nutty ones like fig and almond roll.

Corsica, still not entirely tamed, with the fragrant wild scrub-plants (the *maquis*) perfuming every hillside, has some ways with food that are entirely individual. They make a distinctive flour from sweet chestnuts, for instance. Juniper berries and wild mint are used an unexpected variety of dishes such as *omelette au brocciu*.

Corsicans are great eaters: a favourite old proverb is *corpu tecchiu, anima consula* (full stomach, soul at peace). Other often rich and heavy specialties are *lonzu*, well seasoned, pickled and rolled pork, *prizuttu*, cured ham, a spicy sausage made with liver and pork tongue, and *stufatu*, a macaroni pudding with mushrooms, onions, herbs and cheese. Fish dishes include aromatic stews such as one combining crayfish, tomatoes and peppers.

Corsica is particularly famed for its goatcheese, *brocciu*, which can be eaten fresh and still mild, or mature, when its flavour has sharpened. They also produce a delicious variety of Roquefort. The chestnut flour is used in a great many cakes and pastries: *castagnacci* (tartlets), *fritelles* (doughnuts), and *pisticchini* (sweet soufflés). Rugged though the island may be, even the simplest inn in a remote village seems able to produce an unusual and filling meal at very short notice. ■

■ FISH STEW with CREAMY PEPPER SAUCE

- *1 hour*
- *Serves 4-6*

800 g (1 3/4 lb) firm white fish such as whiting or halibut, cut across into thick steaks
4 potatoes, peeled and quartered
2 onions, sliced
3 garlic cloves, crushed
15 mL (1 tbls) salt
freshly ground black pepper
1 L (4 1/2 cups) boiling water
60 mL (4 tbls) olive oil
bouquet garni of parsley, celery, fennel or dill, lemon zest and bay leaf
8 thin slices of French bread, baked in a low oven until crisp but not browned
Parmesan
15 mL (1 tbls) chopped parsley

■ FOR THE ROUILLE SAUCE
2 thick slices stale French bread, crusts removed

10 mL (2 tsp) paprika
2-5 mL (1/2-1 tsp) red hot pepper sauce
2 garlic cloves, crushed
150 mL (5/8 cup) olive oil
salt

● Combine the fish, potatoes, onions, garlic, salt and pepper in a heavy saucepan. Pour in the boiling water, add the oil and bouquet garni and simmer for about 20 minutes.

● Meanwhile, make the sauce. Soak the bread in cold water and squeeze it dry immediately. Put the bread in a mortar with the chopped chilli and garlic and pound steadily, adding the oil very gradually as for mayonnaise. Finish with 15 mL (1 tbls) of the fish cooking liquid, season with salt and reserve.

● Divide the fish, vegetables and liquid between individual warmed soup bowls. Float two slices of French bread in each and top each slice with a spoonful of the sauce. Sprinkle with parsley and Parmesan and serve.

Fish stew with creamy pepper sauce

■ SKEWERED MUSSELS with TOMATO SAUCE

Serve this with crusty French bread and green salad.

- *1 hour*
- *Serves 2*

32 fat mussels, about 1.5 kg (3 lb)
1 egg yolk
15 mL (1 tbls) milk
4 slices of streaky bacon, cut across
 into 5 cm (2 in) pieces
dried white breadcrumbs,
 preferably home-made

salt and freshly ground black
 pepper
15 mL (1 tbls) olive oil
lemon wedges

■ FOR THE SAUCE
30 mL (2 tbls) tomato paste
30 mL (2 tbls) olive oil
396 mL (14 oz) canned tomatoes
1 bay leaf

Skewered mussels with tomato sauce

5 mL (1 tsp) chopped basil
5 mL (1 tsp) chopped parsley
5 mL (1 tsp) chopped thyme
1 garlic clove, crushed
salt
paprika to taste

● Make the sauce by stirring the tomato paste and oil together in a small heavy saucepan over medium heat. Add the tomatoes and herbs, stir well and bring to simmering point. Let the sauce cook gently, stirring gently, uncovered, for 45 minutes, stirring occasionally.
● Scrub the mussels well, discarding any with open or crushed shells, and put them in a deep saucepan. Cover and shake the pan, without water, over high heat for about 3 minutes. Remove the bodies from the shells.
● Beat the egg yolk and milk together. Thread 4 skewers; start with a square of bacon followed by two mussels and repeat until all the mussels and bacon pieces are used. Dip them in the egg mixture, roll them in the breadcrumbs, season lightly and put them aside for 10 minutes.
● Heat the grill to high. Add the crushed garlic to the sauce, stir well to pulp the tomatoes and season to taste. Remove from the heat and reserve.
● Drip a little olive oil over the skewers and grill them for about 5-7 minutes, turning to cook evenly, until they are golden brown. Serve at once, decorated with the lemon wedges, with the sauce served in a sauce-boat.

*Serve with a chilled rosé,
from Provence or another region.*

■ COURGETTES in HERB TOMATO SAUCE

• *1 hour*
• *Serves 4-6*

1 kg (2.2 lb) small zucchinis, halved lengthways
salt for sprinkling
30 mL (2 tbls) olive oil
2 onions, chopped
30 mL (2 tbls) tomato paste
2 garlic cloves, crushed
796 mL (28 oz) canned peeled tomatoes
5 mL (1 tbls) chopped fresh basil or 7 mL (1 1/2 tsp) dried basil
5 mL (1 tbls) chopped fresh tarragon or 5 mL (1/2 tsp) dried tarragon
salt and freshly ground black pepper

● Sprinkle the cut sides of the zucchinis lightly with salt and set aside to "sweat" while making the sauce.

● Heat the olive oil in a saucepan over low heat and stir in the onions, tomato paste, garlic, tomatoes and basil chervil. Cook gently, uncovered, for about 10 minutes, then season to taste.

● Heat the oven to 200 °C (400 °F). Wipe the zucchinis dry with absorbent paper and arrange them in a shallow ovenproof dish. Cover with the tomato sauce and bake them in the oven for 20-25 minutes. Sprinkle with the chopped tarragon before serving hot. They may also be served cold, sprinkled with tarragon; they then make a lovely contrast to hot dishes.

■ NIÇOIS ONION FLAN

- *30 minutes + cooking: 1 hour 10 minutes*
- *Serves 4*

300 g (10 oz) frozen bread dough, thawed
oil for greasing

■ FOR THE FILLING
700 g (1 1/2 lb) onions, thinly sliced
105 mL (7 tbls) olive oil
10 canned anchovy fillets
10 black olives, pitted
2 pieces of canned sweet red pepper

Niçois onion flan

● ●

dried basil
salt and freshly ground black
    pepper
1 garlic clove, finely chopped

● Leave the dough in a warm place to rise for 2 hours.

● Meanwhile, make the filling. Put the onions into 60 mL (4 tbls) of the oil in a large frying-pan over very low heat. Turn them with a wooden spoon until they are very oily, cover and let the onions soften and become transparent, turning them occasionally to keep them from browning.

● Rinse the anchovy fillets and pat them dry on absorbent paper.

● When the dough has risen, turn it into a floured board, knead for 1 minute and roll it into a ball. Oil a 20 cm (8 in) spring form pan, place the ball of dough in the centre and press it outwards and upwards with your fingers to fit.

● Season the onions with salt and pepper and dried basil to taste, stir in the chopped garlic and press the mixture into the flan. Arrange the anchovy fillets like the spokes of a wheel on top, with the olives between them and, if desired, make a "hub" with an olive. Chop the pepper and sprinkle on top, drizzle with the remaining oil. Heat the oven to 200 °C (400 °F).

● Let the flan rise again for 15 minutes, then set it on a baking sheet in the centre of the oven and bake for 20 minutes. Turn the heat down to 180 °C (350 °F) and bake for a further 15-20 minutes. Serve warm or cold.

■ CORSICAN CHEESE OMELETTE

The faint overtone of mint gives this omelette a unique flavour.

- *15 minutes*
- *Serves 2*

5 eggs
8 leaves fresh mint, finely
    chopped
salt and freshly ground black
    pepper
15 mL (1 tbls) olive oil
25 mL (1 tbls) butter
75 g (3 oz) Brocciu or other fresh
    goat's cheese, sliced
chopped parsley to garnish
    (optional)

● Beat the eggs, 15 mL (1 tbls) cold water and mint together in a bowl until fluffy, and season with the salt and pepper.

● Heat the oil in a large omelette pan, add the butter, swirl and, when the mixture is shimmering-hot, quickly pour in the egg mixture.

● When half-set, arrange the cheese slices on the omelette. When they start to soften fold it over, garnish, if desired, and serve.

■ RASPBERRY CHARLOTTE

A rich and delicious yet simple dessert, the recipe can be adapted to any sharp-tasting fruit such as oranges, lemons or redcurrants.

- *1 hour 15 minutes,*
  plus at least 6 hours chilling
- *Serves 6-8*

700 g (1 1/2 lb) fresh or frozen raspberries
500 mL (2 cups) icing sugar plus extra for dusting
15 mL (1 tbls) gelatine
600 mL (2 1/2 cups) 35% cream
butter for greasing
36 sponge fingers (3 packets of boudoir biscuits)
extra raspberries to garnish (optional)

● Put half of the raspberries with 30 mL (2 tbls) sugar and 45 mL (3 tbls) water in a small saucepan and cook them over low heat for 5 minutes. Press the mixture through a sieve, sprinkle the gelatine on top of the still-hot liquid, whisk, then allow it to stand.

● Whip the cream until thick but not too stiff and dry. Reserve 30 mL (2 tbls) in a piping bag fitted with a rosette nozzle for decorating, if desired. Gradually incorporate first the remaining sugar, then the cooled gelatine mixture into the cream. Fold in the rest of the raspberries.

● Line the bottom and sides of a lightly buttered 1 L (4 1/2 cups) charlotte mould with the sponge fingers, sugar side out. Spoon the fruit and cream mixture into the centre.

● Cover the top with the remaining few sponge fingers cut in half lengthways, and chill for at least 6 hours. Unmould and decorate the centre with a rosette of cream and extra raspberries if desired. Dust with a little icing sugar before serving.

Raspberry charlotte

ROUSSILLON

Sandwiched between Languedoc in south-west France, the Pyrenees and the Mediterranean, lies Roussillon. Fiercely independant and proud of their long history, its peoples have retained their individualistic style of cooking, which is characterised by the liberal use of olive oil, tomatoes, eggplants and garlic.

Roussillon, once called "the centre of the world" by Salvator Dali, is too often neglected or simply lumped together with its neighbouring county, the Languedoc. However, this is Catalan country with a his-

tory, language and culture of its own. Once part of the long-forgotten kingdom of Mallorca, then ceded to the independant province of Catalonia, Roussillon still retains many of its ancient Catalan traditions, despite being part of France since the 17th century. The local language is Catalan, the architecture is Spanish in style and many of the traditions – like the Easter procession of penitents in Perpignan, the capital – recall the festivals of Spain. The area is a mixture of ancient and modern. Tiny villages, where times has stood still,

Sardine fisherman, Collioure

cling precariously to the mountainsides, while on the coast, holiday resorts have been developed with stylish dramatic complexes sweeping round the bays.

Bounded on the south by the Pyrenees, and on the west by the little principality of Andorra, the region may be divided into two. Farthest west is the Cerdagne, a high plateau surrounded by mountains straddling the Franco-Spanish border. Once independant from the rest of Roussillon, and with different food resources from the flat plain and eastern seashore, the Cerdagne has many specialties of its own.

Most famous of these is the substantial thick cabbage, pork, haricot bean and game soup, *braou bouffat* ("good eating"). Partridge with morel is another specialty. A rare and highly prized little black variety abounds in spring on the edge of woods in the mountainous country. Cerdagne is one of the few regions where another rare and delicious dish *civet d'isard* (mountain goat) may be found. The only Catalan habit not much represented here is the use of a great deal of fruit in the kitchen, because the altitude is too high. A few grapes, apples and pears are grown, however, and these are of excellent quality.

Travelling towards the Mediterranean, down through the chestnut forests and lush pasture lands, one reaches the agricultural heart of Catalan country. From here come France's cherries of the year, spring peas and the beautiful white peaches from Île-sur-Tet. Continuing on towards Perpignan, fruits and vegetables flourish in abundance and profusion. Melons, golden peaches and apricots, more cherries, apples and pears grow alongside the vegetables which so dominate the cooking: huge glossy eggplants, enormous, perfect round tomatoes, large purple onions and the fattest heads of garlic ever seen!

Garlic and olive oil are much beloved by the Roussillon people and are eaten even first thing in the morning. A typical Catalan breakfast will be slices of bread rubbed with a garlic clove and moistened with olive oil. The description *à la catalane* after a dish listed on a menu or in a cook book will mean either that it contains at least a whole head of garlic, as in *saucisses à la catalane*, or that the food is sautéed in oil and accompanied by diced eggplants and a pilaff of rice soaked in tomato sauce.

Moving on down towards the coast, where the sun shines in generous measure, the emphasis turns naturally to fish. Sardines, anchovies, fresh tuna and spiny lobsters are the most popular, with grilled snails served to start a meal. Fresh anchovies in particular are much loved, especially when fried in oil with crushed garlic and finely chopped parsley and then stuffed into a brioche. Anchovies are difficult to find outside the ports where they are fished, but fresh sardines can be used in the dish equally well. Salted anchovy fillets appear in many dishes, often in pâté for stuffing potatoes (see recipe) or layered with tomatoes and olives in a light puff pastry to provide a baked savoury. Tuna is braised in fish stock and often eaten cold with *sauce collioures – aïoli* plus anchovy.

Sweets of the area are often sticky and very sweet, suggesting a Moorish influence, like the ring-shaped cake, *touron*, made from egg white, crushed almonds and ground pistachios. Otherwise the sweets are based on the local fruit, like *abricots meringués*. The vineyards here are the oldest in France, dating from the 7th century BC. Côtes du Roussillon is an *Appellation Contrôlée* wine, now widely exported. ■

■ PYRENEAN CHESNUT SOUP

- *Roasting the partridge and making stock, then 3 hours*
- *Serves 4*

1 cold, roasted partridge, wood pigeon or small chicken
700 g (1 1/2 lb) fresh chesnuts
1 large Spanish onion, washed and quartered with the skin left on
bouquet garni (thyme, oregano, parsley)
2 bay leaves
12 white peppercorns
strips of lemon zest
hot croutons fried in olive oil, to serve

● Remove the breast and as much as possible of the rest of the flesh from poultry. Chop it finely and reserve.

● Put the carcass unto a large saucepan, cover with 1.5 L (6 cups) cold water and add the onion, bouquet garni, bay leaves, white peppercorns and lemon zest. Bring to the boil, then reduce the heat and simmer, covered, for 1 1/2 - 2 hours.

● Meanwhile, make a slit in each chestnut on the rounded side, put them on a baking tray and heat under the broiler for 15-20 minutes. (The shells will open at the slits, making it easy to remove the nuts and peel away the inner brown skin.) Hold the nuts in a cloth while shelling and skinning them as they will be hot.

● Strain the stock and return it to the rinsed-out pan to cook over high heat until reduced to 850 mL (3 1/2 cups).

● Add the shelled chestnuts to the stock and simmer gently for 2 hours. Cool slightly then put the mixture in a blender or food processor, together with the chopped meat, and blend thoroughly.

● Return the soup to the pan, season with salt and freshly ground black pepper, and bring it just to the boil.

● Pour the soup into a warmed soup tureen, garnish with the croutons and serve.

■ TUNA in ANCHOVY MAYONNAISE

- *15 minutes, then 30 minutes cooking plus 1 hour cooling*
- *Serves 4*

4 x 175 g (6 oz) fresh tuna or cod steaks
about 600 mL (2 1/2 cups) fish stock
1 crisp lettuce, to serve

■ FOR THE SAUCE
150 mL (1/2 cup) mayonnaise
6 anchovy fillets
15 mL (1 tbls) finely chopped parsley
1 garlic clove, crushed

● Put the fish steaks in a large shallow pan in which they fit comfortably in one layer. Cover with the fish stock and bring to the boil over medium heat. Turn the heat to low, cover the pan and simmer gently for 30 minutes (20 minutes for cod) or until the fish will flake easily with a fork. Turn off the heat and let the steaks cool in the cooking liquid, about 1 hour.

● Meanwhile, pound the anchovy fillets and the garlic in a mortar to a smooth paste. Add this to the mayonnaise, blending well, then stir in the parsley.

● Shred the lettuce finely and spread it over a long serving platter. Drain the steaks well, arrange them on top of the lettuce and mask with the anchovy mayonnaise. Serve immediately.

■ DEEP-FRIED POTATOES with ANCHOVY STUFFING

- *45 minutes*
- *Serves 6*

30 small, even-sized new potatoes
olive oil for deep frying
150 mL (5/8 cup) butter, softened
10 anchovy fillets
parsley sprigs, to garnish

● Scrape the potatoes and wash them thoroughly. Trim a small slice off the bottom of each one so that they can stand upright, then with an apple corer or small sharp pointed knife, dig out about a third of each potato from the opposite end so that there is a small cavity at the top of each potato. Put the prepared potatoes in a bowl of cold water to soak while you prepare the pâté.

● Pound the anchovy fillets add the softened butter, whisking well so that they

are thoroughly blended. Put the pâté in the refrigerator to firm up.

● Heat a large saucepan with 5 cm (2 in) of olive oil to 190 °C (375 °F) or until a cube of stale bread will fry to golden-brown in 50 seconds.

● Quickly pat the potatoes dry and add them to the pan. Cook them for 10-15 minutes until they are golden-brown (the time will vary slightly according to the size and type of the potatoes). Remove them with a slotted spoon and drain on absorbent paper. Let them cool for 2 minutes.

● Arrange the potatoes standing upright on individual serving plates and garnish with parsley sprigs. Quickly fill each potato with about 2.5 mL (1/2 tsp) of the pâté, sprinkle them with freshly ground black pepper and serve immediately.

■ CATALAN BRAISED BEEF

• *4 hours*
• *Serves 6*

1.4 kg (3 lb) top round or top rump, rolled and tied
45 mL (3 tbls) olive oil
1 large Spanish onion, chopped
30 mL (2 tbls) seasoned flour
300 mL (1 1/4 cup) dry white wine
300 mL (1 1/4 cup) button mushrooms, washed but left whole
2 tomatoes, coarsely chopped
2 heads of garlic, cloves peeled but left whole
salt and freshly ground black pepper

● Heat the oven to 150 °C (300 °F). Heat the olive oil in a flameproof casserole, add the onion and sauté for 5 minutes.

● Roll the meat in the seasoned flour, then add it to the casserole and brown it on all sides over a high heat.

● Add the white wine, stir for 2-3 minutes, then add the mushrooms, chopped tomatoes, garlic cloves, a little salt and lots of freshly ground black pepper. Cover and cook in the oven for 3 1/2 hours.

● Transfer the meat to a heated serving platter, remove the string and carve into thick slices. Keep them warm.

● Put the casserole over medium heat and boil the sauce for 4-5 minutes until it is really thick. Spoon some of the sauce over the slices of meat and serve the rest separately in a sauce-boat.

Catalan braised beef

■ PARTRIDGES with SEVILLE ORANGES

Small, bitter oranges grow profusely in Roussillon and are much used with game. Use Seville oranges, or sweet oranges and add the juice of a lemon.

- *Making stock, then 2 hours*
- *Serves 4*

Partridges with Seville oranges

4 young partridges or Cornish hens
60 mL (4 tbls) olive oil
1 onion, finely chopped
30 mL (2 tbls) flour
175 mL (3/4 cup) semi-dry white
    wine
8 Seville oranges or 4 regular
    oranges, peeled with all pits
    removed
juice of 2 Seville oranges or juice of
    1 sweet orange and juice of
    1 lemon
250 mL (1 cup) chicken stock
1 bouquet garni (thyme, marjoram,
    parsley)
2 bay leaves
6 garlic cloves, peeled but whole
200 g (7 oz) canned pimentos,
    drained and sliced
salt and freshly ground black
    pepper
sprigs of watercress, to garnish
lightly cooked green beans,
    to serve

● Heat the olive oil in a large heavy-based saucepan over a medium-high heat and sauté the onion for 4-5 minutes. Remove them with a slotted spoon and reserve.

● Add the partridge and brown on all sides. Stir in the flour and cook for 2-3 minutes.

● Pour in the wine, let it bubble for 2 minutes, then stir to thicken slightly.

● Add the oranges, orange juice, chicken stock, bouquet garni, bay leaves, garlic cloves and reserved onion. Cover with a tightly fitting lid, turn the heat down to very low and simmer gently for 1 hour.

● Add the pimentos to the pan, stirring them well in, cover the pan again and cook for a further 20-30 minutes – the oranges should be very soft and have absorbed as much of the sauce as they can.

● Season to taste. Transfer to a warm serving dish, garnish and serve immediately with lightly cooked green beans.

■ APRICOT and RICE MERINGUE

- *Overnight soaking, then 1 hour 20 minutes*
- *Serves 6*

450 g (1 lb) fresh ripe apricots or 350 g (12 oz) dried apricots soaked overnight in water to cover
25 mL (1 1/2 tbls) butter
125 mL (1/2 cup) short-grain rice
500 mL (2 cups) milk
1 vanilla bean or 5 mL (1 tsp) vanilla extract
300 mL (1 1/4 cup) sugar

2 eggs, separated
15 mL (1 tbls) icing sugar

● If using dried apricots, put them with the soaking liquid into a large pan with the butter and bring them to the boil over medium heat. Turn the heat to low and simmer, covered, for 1 hour until the apricots are very tender and all the liquid has been absorbed. If using fresh ones, just cover with water, bring to the boil with the butter and simmer until very tender, about 10 minutes. Drain the fresh apricots and reserve them.

Apricot and rice meringue

● Wash the rice thoroughly in a sieve under running hot water. Bring a large pan of cold water to the boil and drop in the rice. Boil for 3 minutes, then drain.

● Bring the milk to the boil in a large saucepan with the vanilla bean or vanilla extract, add the rice, reduce the heat and simmer very gently for 20 minutes.

● Add 125 mL (1/2 cup) of the sugar to the rice and simmer for another 25 minutes, stirring occasionally to prevent the rice from sticking.

● Turn the rice into a shallow, oval ovenproof serving dish, let it cool for 2 minutes, then beat in the 2 egg yolks. Heat the oven to 180 °C (350 °F).

● Put the apricots in a layer on top of the rice.

● Whisk the egg whites in a large bowl until stiff peaks form. Carefully fold in the remaining sugar with a metal spoon, then spoon the meringue mixture into a piping bag fitted with a 1.5 cm (1/2 in) plain nozzle.

● Pipe the meringue in a lattice pattern over the apricots, sprinkle with the icing sugar and bake in the oven for 15 minutes.

● Turn the oven up to 220 °C (425 °F) and bake for a further 5 minutes. Remove from the oven and serve hot, warm or cold.

■ SAUSAGES "à la CATALANE"

- *1 hour 15 minutes*
- *Serves 4*

2 heads of garlic, peeled but left whole
900 g (2 lb) long, thin soft pork sausage
30 mL (2 tbls) lard
15 mL (1 tbls) flour
15 mL (1 tbls) dry white wine
250 mL (1 cup) canned or home made chicken consommé
30 mL (2 tbls) tomato purée
5 mL (1 tsp) dried thyme
5 mL (1 tsp) dried tarragon
15 mL (1 tbls) freshly chopped parsley
10 cm (4 in) strip of orange zest
5 mL (1 tsp) lemon juice

● Put the lard in a flameproof casserole or heavy-based saucepan and brown the sausage over a medium heat for 3-4 minutes. Remove from the pan and reserve.

● Add the flour to the pan and stir to make a roux. Pour in the white wine and stir until it thickens slightly. Add the consommé and tomato paste, bring to the boil then lower the heat and simmer gently for 15 minutes.

● Return the sausage to the pan, together with the garlic cloves, herbs, orange zest and lemon juice. Stir well to cover the sausage with sauce, then cover the pan and simmer for another 30 minutes.

● Remove the sausage from the pan and arrange it on a large round serving platter coiled up like a garden hose. Pour over the sauce and serve it immediately.

■ EGGPLANT with EGG STUFFING

- *1 hour 10 minutes*
- *Serves 2-4*

1 large eggplant
1 onion, finely chopped
125 mL (1/2 cup) olive oil
1 hard-boiled egg, shelled and
finely chopped
45 mL (3 tbls) dried white
breadcrumbs
45 mL (3 tbls) finely chopped
parsley
2 garlic cloves, crushed
salt and freshly ground black
pepper

● Slice the eggplant in half lengthways, sprinkle each half with salt and leave them to stand for 30 minutes.

● Meanwhile, heat 30 mL (2 tbls) olive oil in a heavy-based saucepan over low heat, add the onion and cook gently for 30 minutes until they are very soft and mushy. Heat the oven to 180 °C (350 °F).

● Remove the onion from the pan with a slotted spoon and reserve in a large bowl. Wash the eggplant thoroughly in cold water to remove all traces of salt.

● Add 75 mL (5 tbls) of the olive oil to the pan over medium-low heat and sauté the eggplant for 15 minutes turning them 3 or 4 times during cooking. Remove the eggplant from the pan and carefully scoop out the flesh with a small spoon, adding it to the bowl with the onion.

● Add the finely chopped hard-boiled egg, 30 mL (2 tbls) of the breadcrumbs, the parsley and crushed garlic cloves. Season to taste with salt and pepper and mix everything together well.

● Carefully pile the stuffing into the eggplant shells and put them on an ovenproof serving dish. Sprinkle the remaining breadcrumbs over, dampen the tops with the remaining oil and bake them for 20 minutes. Serve immediately.

BOURBONNAIS, AUVERGNE and LYONNAIS

The mouth-watering cooking in the area of France around and north of Lyons takes in the simple dishes of the Bourbonnais and Auvergne regions as well as the more elaborate ones of the area around Lyons. Among them are the Bourbonnais cabbage and walnut soup, the potato-cheese dishes of the Auvergne and the Lyonnais' famous onion-flavoured ones.

Bourbonnais, nestling in the centre of France, is sometimes called the gateway to Auvergne. It was once said of the Bourbonnais peasants that they were proud, poverty-stricken and greedy. They certainly have always eaten well. Their cooking is essentially simple, but the ingredients are particularly fine. These include plump chick-

ens and geese and Charolais beef, which is known world-wide for its excellence.

A wide variety of vegetables is grown and vegetable dishes are highly prized by the Bourbonnais. Vegetable *gratins* are very popular and may consist of whatever vegetables are in season; one delicious sauce used to coat them is lemon-flavoured white sauce incorporating gently sautéed onion and grated Gruyère cheese.

Soups are based on vegetables or walnuts, another specialty. It would be fair to suppose that the iced leek soup, Vichyssoise, is a regional French soup from the town of Vichy which is in the Bourbonnais. In fact it was created in far away New York by a French chef, Louis

Farmers near Lyons

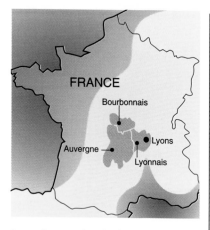

FRANCE

Bourbonnais

Lyons

Auvergne

Lyonnais

Diat, who named it after his native town.

Walnut oil is quite frequently used for cooking in preference to olive oil as walnut trees are a great feature of the landscape, as are chestnut trees.

Tourtes are to be found in most *départements*, but the most famous in this area is a double crust potato cake or *tourton*. Another variety is made with a stuffing, of pork and veal mixed, very highly seasoned, and filled after cooking with melted pork fat poured in through a funnel. Eaten cold, it is rather like an English raised pork pie. These *tourtes* are favoured in the Montluçon region from which come the most delicious pears. It is interesting that recipes which elsewhere use apples, here are prepared with dessert pears, as in the excellent pear turnovers, or *chaussons*.

Once in the neighbouring Auvergne, the countryside becomes mountainous and the cooking perhaps more simple than in Bourbonnais. Yet Auvergne is justly famous for its pastry, *charcuterie* and filling dishes. One of these, *aligot*, is made with cooked, whipped potatoes and the local robust Cantal cheese. The same cheese is used in the main course bread, onion and cheese soup, *soupe de cantal*.

Although tourists visit this rough, wild region of France perhaps less often than others, its cheeses are exported and respected worldwide. Besides delicious Cantal, Auvergne is renowned for cheeses such as Saint-Nectaire, fresh mild *tomme*, dry goat cheeses and the assertive but heavenly *bleu d'Auvergne*.

Further to the east is the Lyonnais, a small province with an impressive culinary reputation. Some say that Lyons is the capital city of the French table. Accessible to it are the riches of Bresse, Burgundy, Charolais and the valley of the Rhône. Reigning above all in Lyonnais cuisine is the onion. The citizens of Lyons say that Parisian onion soup is only an adaptation of Lyonnais onion soup which is thickened with rice and is not poured over cheese toasts, like the Parisian onion soup.

Many of the Lyonnais restaurants which uphold the tradition of fine food were, and still are, owned and run by female chefs. The most famous one, perhaps, was Mère (mother) Fillioux, who ran her renowned kitchen after World War I.

The *pot au feu à la lyonnaise*, made with beef, is unusual in that it is thickened with dried peas and served with red cabbage. Beef is by far the favourite meat in Lyons, including the tail. Eminent Lyonnais chefs such as Paul Bocuse cook for large parties such grandiose dishes as whole leg of beef simmered in an immense cauldron whith chickens, sausages, joints of veal and game birds.

To complete a gourmet meal in Lyons, one might be served a rich chestnut pudding. A typical old country recipe calls for three dozen sweet chestnuts cooked with a hint of cloves, then sieved and combined with vanilla-flavoured sugar, softened butter and egg yolks. Gently whisked egg whites are folded in and the mixture is turned into a well-buttered mould. It is sprinkled with pistachio nuts and baked in a cool oven and serve as an exquisite dessert. ■

■ HARD-BOILED EGGS LYONNAISE-STYLE

- *About 30 minutes*
- *Serves 4*

8 eggs, hard-boiled
2 onions, sliced
60 mL (1/4 cup) butter
1 garlic clove, crushed
500 mL (2 cups) hot milk
salt and freshly ground white
    pepper
butter for greasing
100 g (4 oz) Gruyère cheese,
    thinly sliced
crusty French bread, to serve

● Cut the onions in very thin slices. Put them in a clean tea-towel, twist the ends firmly and immerse the part containing the onions in a pan of boiling water for 20 seconds. Lift it out and twist the ends of the cloth further to wring excess water from the onions.

● Melt the butter in a pan over medium heat, add the prepared onions and stir gently for 1 minute. Add the garlic and pour over the milk, stirring well. Season and cook, stirring, until the onions are tender.

● Heat the oven to broil. Shell and thickly slice the eggs. Arrange them in a well-buttered ovenproof dish and spoon the onion mixture over. Cover with overlapping slices of cheese and place under the hot grill for about 5 minutes, or until the cheese melts and bubbles. Serve hot with bread.

Gruyère cheese

■ BAKED CARP with HERBS

By tradition, the dish containing the carp was sealed with a flour and water dough which was broken off and discarded when the fish was cooked. Nowadays foil, well crimped under the edge of the dish, is used and makes the recipe much simpler to prepare.

- 2 hours 15 minutes
- Serves 4

butter for greasing
1 large carrot, sliced
1 large onion, sliced
2 shallots, chopped

1 garlic clove, crushed
2 bay leaves
5 mL (1 tsp) dried thyme
15 mL (1 tbls) chopped parsley
salt and freshly ground black
    pepper
1.5 kg (3 1/4 lb) carp, scaled and
    cleaned

Ingredients for baked carp with herbs

54

60 mL (4 tbls) wine vinegar
60 mL (4 tbls) olive oil plus extra
  for greasing

■ FOR SERVING AND GARNISHING
**4 large oval croutons, about 10 cm
(4 in) in length, fried in butter
parsley sprigs and lemon wedges**

● Heat the oven to 150 °C (300 °F).
Generously grease a shallow ovenproof
dish just large enough to take the fish
and vegetables comfortably, and
arrange the vegetables and herbs in it.
Sprinkle lightly with salt and pepper.
Lay the fish on top, pour over the
vinegar and oil and add enough cold
water to come about half-way up the
fish. Cover tightly with greased foil
and cook in the oven for 2 hours.

● Arrange the croutons on a warm
serving platter. Lift out the fish carefully
with 2 spatulas and allow it to drain
well. Place the fish on the croutons and
garnish with sprigs of parsley and lemon
wedges.

● Strain the juices from the cooking dish
into a warm sauce-boat, add salt and
pepper if necessary and serve the fish
immediately, with the sauce handed
separately.

> *Choose a dry white wine,
> for example, an Alsacian Riesling.*

■ SAUSAGES with WINE and CHEESE

*Cervelas are highly seasoned meaty
sausages and are available in two sizes;
the larger sausages serve two people
each.*

- *About 45 minutes*
- *Serves 4*

**4 small Cervelas sausages
butter for greasing
125 mL (1/2 cup) white wine
175 mL (3/4 cup) Gruyère cheese,
  grated
flat-leaved parsley, to garnish
green salad, to serve
crusty bread, to serve**

● Prick the sausages with a fork and
poach them in simmering water just to
cover for 30 minutes.
● Meanwhile, heat the oven to 220 °C
(425 °F). Drain the sausages and cut
each one in half lengthways. Arrange
the pieces of sausage, cut surfaces
downwards, in a greased shallow
ovenproof dish. Spoon the wine over
and sprinkle with the cheese. Bake in
the oven for 10 minutes. Arrange
flat-leaved parsley leaves between the
cervelas halves to garnish, then serve
the sausages hot from the ovenproof
dish with a green salad crusty bread.

To make a substantial main dish, the
sliced Cervelas sausages can be served
on a bed of cooked lentils delicately
flavoured with bay leaves and thyme,
dotted with buttter and sprinkled with
salt and pepper.

■ CHICKEN in CHEESE SAUCE

- *1 hour 45 minutes*
- *Serves 4*

1.4 kg (3 lb) chicken
salt and freshly ground black pepper
25 mL (1 1/2 tbls) butter, at room
temperature
300 mL (1 1/4 cup) hot Bechamel

■ SAUCE
300 mL (1 1/4 cup) Gruyère cheese,
grated
60 mL (1/4 cup) 35% cream,
whipped

● Heat the oven to 190 °C (375 °F).
Season the chicken inside and out with salt
and pepper. Spread the butter over the
chicken, put it in a roasting tin and cook
for 1 hour and 20 minutes.

● Meanwhile, make the sauce, season
strongly with pepper and keep hot.

● Divide the cooked chicken into quarters
and arrange these, skin side upwards, in
a *gratin* dish.

● Stir 3/4 of the cheese into the sauce,
then fold in the cream. Spoon the sauce
over the chicken portions to coat them,
then sprinkle with the remaining cheese.
Heat the grill to medium-high.

● Put the dish under the hot grill for
about 5 minutes, or until the cheese is
bubbling and golden brown.
Serve immediately.

Hot Bechamel
for chicken
in cheese sauce

■ OXTAIL and ONION STEW

- *Making stock, plus 2 hours soaking, then 4 hours*
- *Serves 4*

1 large oxtail, skinned and cut
    into 5 cm (2 in) pieces
45 mL (3 tbls) seasoned flour
45 mL (3 tbls) lard
3 onions, sliced
1 large carrot, sliced
3 garlic cloves, crushed
30 mL (2 tbls) *marc de Bourgogne*
    or brandy
250 mL (1 cup) dry red wine
250 mL (1 cup) beef stock
30 mL (2 tbls) tomato paste
1 bouquet garni
3 strips of pork skin, blanched
salt and freshly ground black
    pepper
8 canned chestnuts
boiled potatoes, to serve

● Soak the pieces of oxtail in cold water to cover for at least 2 hours. Drain, put them in a large pan, cover with fresh water and bring to the boil, skimming if necessary. Drain well and coat with seasoned flour.

● Heat the oven to 150 °C (300 °F). Melt the lard in a large flameproof casserole, add the onion, carrot and pieces of oxtail and fry over medium heat, stirring occasionally, until the onion is golden.

● Add the garlic, *marc* or brandy, wine, stock, tomato paste, bouquet garni, pork strips and a little seasoning. Bring to the boil, stirring, then cover and place in the oven for 3 hours.

● Skim the excess fat from the surface of the stew and adjust the seasoning if necessary. Stir in the chestnuts, cover the dish again and return to the oven for a further 20 minutes. Discard the bouquet garni. Serve with boiled potatoes.

● ●

PEAR BATTER PUDDING

- *About 1 hour*
- *Serves 4*

125 mL (1/2 cup) flour
45 mL (3 tbls) sugar
2 eggs
150 mL (5/8 cup) milk
2 large, firm, ripe pears
60 mL (1/4 cup) butter
sifted icing sugar for sprinkling

● Heat the oven to 220 °C (425 °F). Sift the flour and salt into a bowl, stir in the

sugar and make a well in the centre. Drop in the eggs, add half the milk and whisk until the batter is smooth. Gradually whisk in the remaining milk. Leave the batter to stand for 30 minutes.

● Meanwhile, peel, core and slice the pears. Beat up the batter again and fold in the pears.

● Use half the butter to generously grease a 1 L (4 1/2 cups) ovenproof dish. Pour in the fruit batter and put the remaining butter in slivers on top. Bake in the oven for 30 minutes, or until well risen and golden brown.

● ●

■ RICH HERBED POTATO PIE

- *1 hour 40 minutes*
- *Serves 6*

450 g (1 lb) flour
7 mL (1 1/2 tsp) salt
175 mL (3/4 cup) butter,
   plus extra for greasing
2 large eggs, 1 egg separated
flour for sprinkling

■ FOR THE FILLING
1 kg (2 lb) medium-sized waxy
   potatoes
salt
freshly ground black pepper
60 mL (4 tbls) chopped parsley
250 mL (1 cup) 35% cream, lightly
   whipped

30 mL (2 tbls) chopped chervil or
   10 mL (2 tsp) dried chervil
2 onions, finely chopped

● Sift the flour and salt into a bowl
and rub in the butter until the mixture
resembles breadcrumbs. Whisk one
whole egg and one egg white lightly
with 60 mL (4 tbls) cold water, add this
to the dry ingredients and mix with a
round-bladed knife until the dough
leaves the sides of the bowl clean.
Chill for 20 minutes.

Rich herbed potato pie

● Meanwhile, blanch the potatoes for 5 minutes in a large pan of boiling, salted water. Drain well, and when cool enough to handle, cut them into slices.

● Heat the oven to 200 °C (400 °F). Roll out slightly more than half the pastry on a floured surface, then line a greased 23 cm (9 in) *tourtière* or flan tin.

● Arrange about a third of the potato slices in the pastry case, season lightly with salt and pepper and sprinkle over about half the herbs and shallots. Cover with another third of the potato slices, season and sprinkle with the rest of the herbs and shallots, then cover with the remaining potato.

● Beat the remaining egg yolk with 15 mL (1 tbls) water and brush the pastry edges. Roll out the rest of the pastry to make a lid and cover the pie. Seal the edges well. Brush with the remaining egg yolk. Wash and cut 4 small steam vents spaced evenly in the top of the pie. Bake for 25 minutes, then reduce oven heat to 180 °C (350 °F) and cook for 20 minutes.

● Remove the pie from the oven and open the steam vents sufficiently with a sharp knife to take a small funnel. Pour one quarter of the cream into each of the steam vents and return the pie to the oven for a further 10 minutes, or until the top is rich golden brown. Serve hot.

■ WALNUT-CABBAGE SOUP

This soup owes much of its charm to the delicate flavour of fresh shelled walnuts and walnut oil, but even dried walnuts give good results.

- *About 30 minutes*
- *Serves 4*

10 mL (2 tsp) walnut or peanut oil
450 g (1 lb) shredded light green crinkly cabbage, such as Savoy
3 potatoes, diced
salt
freshly ground black pepper
75 mL (1/3 cup) walnut pieces
15 mL (1 tbls) chopped fresh chervil or 7 mL (1 1/2 tsp) dried chervil
4 slices light rye bread

● Put the oil in a large pan, add the cabbage and potato, stir lightly to coat the vegetables, then cover and put the pan over medium heat, shaking it frequently, for about 1 minute.

● Add 1 L (4 1/2 cups) boiling water, 5 mL (1 tsp) salt and the walnut pieces. Bring back to the boil, stir well, cover and simmer for 20 minutes, or until the cabbage is tender and the potato has virtually disintegrated. Stir in the chervil and season with pepper, adding more salt only if necessary.

● Toast the bread lightly and put one slice in each soup bowl. Ladle the soup over and serve at once. If using dried chervil, add it to the soup with the walnut pieces.

■ PEAR TURNOVERS

- *10 minutes plus 3 hours standing, then 45 minutes*
- *Make 8 turnovers*

4 large ripe, firm pears
125 mL (1/2 cup) sugar
pinch of freshly ground white pepper
1 mL (1/4 tsp) vanilla extract
45 mL (3 tbls) dark rum
60 mL (1/4 cup) 35% cream, whipped

■ FOR THE SWEET DOUGH
1 L (4 1/2 cups) flour
pinch of salt
250 mL (1 cup) butter
15 mL (1 tbls) sugar
flour for dusting
1 egg, beaten

■ TO SERVE
thick cream, whipped

● Peel, halve and core the pears. Chop the flesh finely and put it in a bowl. Sprinkle with the sugar and freshly ground white pepper, add the vanilla extract, rum and whipped cream. Mix the ingredients, cover the bowl and macerate for 3 hours.

● Sift the flour with the salt into a bowl and rub in the butter until the mixture resembles breadcrumbs. Stir in the sugar. Add 60-75 mL (4-5 tbls) cold water to make a firm dough. Chill for 20 minutes.

● Heat the oven to 200 °C (400 °F). Divide the pastry into 8 equal portions and roll out each one on a floured surface to a long oval shape about 18 x 9 cm (7 x 3 1/2 in).

● Spoon the pear filling onto one half of each pastry oval. Brush the pastry edges with egg, fold over to enclose the filling and press to seal the edges firmly.

● Arrange the turnovers on a lightly floured baking sheet and prick each one about six times with a fine skewer. Brush them all over with the remaining beaten egg and bake for about 25 minutes, or until golden.
Serve hot, with thick cream.

Pear turnovers

RECIPES INDEX

■ Vol. 4: CHINA

■ Vol. 5: VIETNAM • JAPAN • THAILAND • KOREA • MALAYSIA • INDONESIA

■ Vol. 6: SPAIN • PORTUGAL • GREECE • EGYPT • MOROCCO

■ Vol. 7: LOUISIANA • CALIFORNIA • MEXICO • SOUTH AMERICA

■ Vol. 8:
SOUTH OF FRANCE

© MARSHALL CAVENDISH 1992.

© TRANSCRIPT PUBLISHING, 395, boul. Lebeau, Saint-Laurent (Québec) H4N 1S2.

Division of Transcontinental Publications Inc. Member of Groupe Transcontinental G.T.C. Ltd.

• General manager: Pierre-Louis Labelle• Marketing manager: Robert Ferland • Administrative assistant: Dominique Denis • Editor in chief: Danielle Champagne • Reviser: Martine Gaudreault • Proofreaders: Services d'édition Guy Connolly • Creative Director: Fabienne Léveillé • Computer graphics designers: Lan Lephan, Badin-Côté Design

Legal Deposit: 4th quarter 1992 - Bibliothèque nationale du Québec - Bibliothèque nationale du Canada